Trading Identities

Why countries and companies are taking on each others' roles

Wally Olins

The Foreign Policy Centre

81908

First published in 1999 by
The Foreign Policy Centre
Panton House
25 Haymarket
London
SW1Y 4EN
T 0171 925 1800
F 0171 925 1811
E info@fpc.org.uk
www.fpc.org.uk

Printed in Great Britain by
Direct Image

Cover design by
Wolff Olins

Trading Identities
Why countries and companies are taking on each others' roles

Acknowledgements

I've been brooding about national identity and global companies on and off for years. And naturally I've wasted a lot of my own and other people's time discussing the subject. Friends and colleagues have given me many insights and much help. Brian Boylan, John Williamson, Jesús Encinar, Hans Arnold and Jonathan Knowles at Wolff Olins have at various times been buttonholed by me and I thank them very much for their observations and their patience.

Mark Leonard, Adam Lury and Sunder Katwala have read and reread drafts and have provided very helpful editing suggestions and ideas. Martin Hansen of Wolff Olins designed the very clever cover and Alice Huang, also of Wolff Olins, made it all happen. I'm very grateful to them too. Jane Houghton and Simone Fletcher have been models in the Personal Assistant department and Dornie Watts has as always given me constant support.

I thank them all.

Wally Olins
London 1999

1. Introduction: Trading Identities

The relationship between countries and companies is changing. In some ways they are becoming more like each other. But in other respects they are beginning to exchange roles. Nations increasingly emphasise nationality; global companies increasingly ignore it. Nations increasingly use business speak – growth targets, education targets, health targets; global companies increasingly emphasise soft issues, their value to society and their benevolent influence. The relationship between companies and countries is getting closer. They compete, they overlap, they swap places.

Perhaps the most significant and most misunderstood manifestation of this phenomenon emerges in the way the nation now attempts to build a brand. Countries are building their national brands as they compete not only for power and influence, but in the new marketing battles for exports, inward investment and tourism.

Until recently countries have always dominated companies. And many companies like Sony in Japan and Coca-Cola in the US derive their personality and strength from their national origins. But these traditional relationships are breaking down. Today 46 out of the top 100 economies are companies, not countries.

As global companies get bigger and more powerful, they are able to move and manufacture across borders, negotiating with the countries and regions which compete for their investment as equals. Global companies are loosening their national ties, developing so many links in so many places that it is impossible to tell where their loyalties lie. They are beginning to ignore nationality among their own staff; they are trying to locate themselves where taxes are lowest and legal constraints are fewest. They are "nation-building" as they seek internal cohesion and popular legitimacy.

And corporate brands are often much better known than nations. Not just Nike, MacDonalds and Coca-Cola, but Mercedes, Microsoft, Apple, Kodak and many others. Leading global companies are economically stronger than many nations. The global sales total for the Ford Motor Company in 1998 was greater than the GDP of Greece, Ireland and Luxembourg combined, and Bill Gates' personal wealth is worth more than 135 countries. And many industries, from telecoms and automobiles to pharmaceuticals, are busy spawning vast enterprises no longer constrained by the nation, whose modest borders, inward looking fiscal restrictions and narrow culture can seem an irrelevance given these companies' global ambitions.

Corporations believe that they can gain the admiration, even affection, of host communities by playing an influential and respected role in each of the countries where they operate. As they merge across frontiers, they seek to legitimise themselves by playing a larger part in the lives of citizens everywhere.

But this does not mean that "companies now rule the world". Nations remain the defining political unit of our age. There are now more nations in the world than ever before – the UN has 185 members today compared to 51 in 1946. The queue of potential new nations from Palestine to Kosovo, Montenegro to East Timor, continues to grow.

But countries are also changing. The primacy of the nation-state seems to be questioned, from above by regional integration from Mercoscur to NAFTA and above all the European Union, and from below as regionalism within Spain, Italy, Belgium, Canada, Britain and elsewhere is now joined by regionalism across nations, like Danish-Swedish Öresund. Countries everywhere are removing themselves from many of their traditional roles in health, education, even security, and letting companies deliver the services instead. While countries face many new pressures, they are developing new strategies for dealing with them, partly by combining regional integration with devolution, a bit like the decentralised management of mega-merged corporations – but also by developing national brands.

Nations continue to attempt to project their political power, but nowadays they also need to compete on hard, quantifiable issues – exports, inward investment and tourism. Each nation now seeks to promote its individual personality, culture, history and values, projecting what may be an idealised but immediately recognisable idea of itself. These pressures drive nations to adopt the marketing and branding techniques used successfully by so many global companies for a long time.

Most countries find this difficult because they are little known. The problem for Belize, Paraguay, Mongolia, Sri Lanka, Gabon and most of the rest of the world's nations is that, outside a very limited sphere, nobody knows or cares anything about them. At the other end of the spectrum, the United States of America stands alone because its world reputation is ubiquitous and overwhelming. Somewhere in the middle are countries like China, India, Russia, Britain and France. Everyone, everywhere has heard of them. But even these perceptions are dominated by caricature – spiritual India, efficient Germany, traditional Britain, passionate Spain and so on – which can hold them back. In fact, it is these well-known but often misunderstood countries which have led the way with national branding projects, even though it is the lesser-known nations who may need to do this even more.

So, as countries and companies face new challenges, they are increasingly learning vital lessons from each other. This pamphlet seeks to show how nations and global companies are changing, emulating each other, taking over each others' roles and competing with each other. It seeks to show how, together, countries and companies are reshaping our ideas about the way the world works.

Part One:
Countries
From nation-state to national brand?

National "branding" is one of the most contentious political concepts of our time. From Spain to Australia, Scandinavia to Singapore, everybody is talking about it. The phenomenon has been especially popular in the British isles – from Celtic Tigers and Rebranding Britain to Cool Cymru and Caledonia – and yet wherever and however it is discussed it is more or less grossly misunderstood and trivialised.

The popular assumption is that national branding is a novel concept, a shallow substitute for more substantive political projects, of concern only to middle-aged politicians anxious to look young and cool. But if the Emperor has no clothes, it is surprising that so many countries have thought it central to their pursuit of prosperity and influence.

In fact, because nations have always competed for power and prestige, branding – although it was never called that – has been an integral element in the competition. Competition between nations today increasingly takes place in three commercial areas – inward investment, tourism and export of goods and services – where success or failure can accurately be charted, and where questions of reputation, image, identity and hence marketing and branding are central to competitive edge.

2. The long history of national branding

Of course, building and remoulding national identities is nothing new. The legends of El Cid and King Arthur, as nation-builders and defenders of the Christian spirit, form part of the national heritage in old countries like Spain and England. Mallory's 15th-century 'Legends of Morte D'Arthur' and Shakespeare's histories were further examples of nation-building in England. While no nation has been immune from inventing traditions, the French are great specialists in it. France's five republics, two empires and about four kingdoms (depending on how you count them) offer a fascinating case-study of how creating and establishing identities has long been a central preoccupation of nations and regimes, and was often highly influential in establishing their legitimacy and their hold on power.

Manufacturing France

The first French Republic changed the flag from the Fleur de Lys to the Tricolore, introduced the Marseillaise as a new national anthem, replaced old weights and measures with the metric system and introduced a new calendar with different names for the months. Even God was replaced by the Supreme Being. You couldn't get much more radical than that.

Napoleon Bonaparte had similarly strong instincts about the way symbolism could sway the nation. Within hours of subverting the Republic and creating an Empire, he awarded the new title 'Marshal of the Empire' to his fourteen most valued commanders whom he would from then on greet as 'mon cousin'. This led the way for a rich panoply of Grand Almoners, Princes, High Constables and a whole string of other titles each with its uniforms, symbols, colours and all with a carefully determined place in a complex hierarchy, quite different from, yet strangely reminiscent of the old Bourbon court. Naturally there was a coronation, and although the Pope came all the way from Rome to Paris, he wasn't allowed to crown the Emperor. Like Pépin and Charlemagne, Napoleon crowned himself, and the Empress too, with the incomparable artist-propandist Jacques-Louis David on hand to immortalise this and other significant events of the epoch.

It is no coincidence that so many of the seminal events of Napoleon's reign have been memorialised. His legend lived on after Waterloo and exile in the South Atlantic. The Arc de Triomphe, built to mark Napoleon's victories, has remained at the heart of French national celebrations, right up to the Liberation and the World Cup victory of 1998. But the political implications of Napoleonic imagery were more immediate. Napoleon's body was brought back from St. Helena and buried in the tomb of Les Invalides during the reign of Louis Philippe (1830-48), who was thrown out in favour of another Napoleon Bonaparte. The Prince President Louis Napoleon became Napoleon III, the second and last French Emperor. Bonapartism played a significant part in bringing him to power and sustaining his position until disastrous defeat by the Prussians in 1870.

The Third Republic emerged from the ashes of the Franco-Prussian war but the deep distrust of Republicanism, associated with Terror, Robespierre and instability, meant it had to steer very cautiously between left and right. And so, from the 1870s onward, the mainly bourgeois government of the Third Republic invented a tradition of admiration, respect and love for the Republican ideal culminating in the parades, processions and celebrations of Bastille Day, invented in 1880, nearly one hundred years after the event itself. The Third Republic continued to reinforce its Republican heritage in state education, exhibitions, and monuments like the Eiffel Tower until its unhappy demise in 1940. Even the puppet Vichy government, under the geriatric leadership of the First World War hero Pétain, reached for symbolism to seek legitimacy, substituting what was by then the traditional French Republican slogan or, as we would say today, strapline, *'liberté, égalité, fraternité'* with *'travail, famille, patrie'*. Other Republican symbols were similarly travestied as the Vichy regime struggled on until the Liberation, and the Fourth Republic's attempts to recreate Republican traditions from the depths to which they had sunk.

De Gaulle, like Napoleon, had a genius for image-making which went well beyond his use of the Cross of Lorraine to rally the Free French in exile. He was out of favour for much of the early post-war period. When at last he came to power, his creation of the Fifth Republic was able to resuscitate and then reinvent elements of both the Republican and Monarchical traditions in France, which had see-sawed through revolution and counter-revolution ever since the Revolution. Delivering democratic stability to France involved creating a new – Presidential – tradition which fuses democracy and powerful symbolism, notable in the *grands projets* of De Gaulle's successors from Pompidou to Mitterrand. For France, the Channel Tunnel is more a symbol of French technological prowess than of practical interest.

And where France led, others followed. Nation-building on a truly significant scale dates from the late 18th and early 19th centuries. Cultural propagandists, from academics, linguists and historians to musicians and painters, deliberately and consciously invented or revived patriotic traditions; this was largely for a domestic audience made captive by universal education and male compulsory military service. The use of myth and history contributed to both national independence and national aggrandisement whose results are, often very uncomfortably, still with us.

Imperial Mission Statements

The propaganda of Empire took this to another level. Britain and France, the two leading imperial powers of the 19th century, both developed constructs, what we would call today 'mission statements', which explained, justified and rationalised their imperial purpose through elaborate propaganda machines projecting the imperial idea. The British Empire was about justice, 'fair play' and the rule of law; the French Empire about *la civilisation Française*. These programmes may not have been consciously co-ordinated, but the ideas behind them gave them coherence and their overall impact was overwhelming. Stamps, coins, monuments, flags and similar physical reminders of the imperial presence were reinforced by primary and secondary education emphasising the superiority of the languages, culture and historical viewpoint of the conquerors.

The international exhibition so popular in the second half of the 19th century was a favoured medium of the national and imperial propagandists, both to raise internal morale and to project the cultural, political and military achievements of the nation to its competitors everywhere else in the world. The Paris Exposition Universelle of 1855 was a direct reply to the Great Exhibition held at the Crystal Palace in 1851. Other exhibitions celebrated great anniversaries, the Philadelphia Centennial of 1876 and the 1889 Paris Universelle, while the Golden and Diamond Jubilees of the Queen-Empress Victoria in Britain were made into occasions of national euphoria, with the might and universal benefits of Empire memorialised by Kipling and others. They were created, as we would say today, by spin-doctors for public consumption, abroad as well as at home.

There were few limits to the scope and scale of nation-building. We think that corporate name changes to reflect a new market positioning and personality are a modern phenomenon, but the House of Saxe Coburg Gotha was relaunched as the House of Windsor during the First World War when Germany was the enemy.

So, throughout history, many nations, political regimes and projects have made the issue of projecting identity a major priority worth time, trouble, money and resources. They continue to do so today, although the arenas in which countries compete for power and influence, their goals in doing so, and so the methods which they use are different. If the old branding projects were aimed at internal audiences – to persuade citizens to pay taxes and fight wars – the new projects are aimed at an external audience – to promote investment, tourism and exports.

3. New pressures on the nation-state: inward investment, export and tourism

The nation-state is not about to disappear – but it operates today in a very different and intensely competitive commercial context. Competition takes place in three areas in which success or failure can accurately be charted – inward investment, tourism and the export of goods and services. Some countries are very successful at some or all of these – others are failures.

An increasingly interdependent global economy means that companies look outside their own borders to find cheaper places to get their products built. US investment in Mexico has led to *maquiladoras*, US-financed Mexican factories paying Mexican wages for products which are then shipped a few kilometres back across the US border for sale. These *maquiladoras* sustain a significant proportion of the Mexican economy. Nations or regions less conveniently located than Mexico have to fight each other hard to get this kind of investment. Every nation and every region wants to capture the biggest slice of inward investment, from the biggest companies, for themselves. And this means, for example, that Wales may compete with Hungary and Portugal to get major investment from a company in the Silicon Valley, which may be equally ignorant of, or prejudiced about, each or all of them (I know a man who works in IT in Silicon Valley, who thinks that Wales swim in the sea). So prejudice and ignorance have to be dispelled through advertising, brochures, websites, competitive tenders, beauty parades, presentations and all the other paraphernalia of modern marketing.

Marketing inward investment properly is a serious, expensive and sophisticated business. It's about presenting a nation or a region in a powerful, attractive and differentiating way. The presentational and promotional techniques required for this type of activity are similar to those required for marketing products or services. Almost all of the regions successful in attracting investment run sophisticated promotional programmes, have networks of offices around the world, and employ professional marketeers. The rewards are vast. Wales, one of the most successful regions in the world in winning inward investment, has attracted a staggering £12.6bn over 16 years.

Then there's export. Corporate brands and the identities of nations from which they derive have always fed off each other and overlapped. For many people, Sony is Japan and Japan is Sony. Germany is cool, unemotional engineering efficiency like Mercedes Benz. Italy is stylish like Max Mara. Britain is traditional like Burberry. But because these national brands tend to reinforce age-old national stereotypes they are inevitably limiting and limited. What about German brands that depend on emotion – Hugo Boss or Wella hair care products? What about British products like Psion which don't have traditional connotations? And what about those nations, some quite big or well-known, which have no brand associations at all? Not just Slovakia or Slovenia, but India, the Philippines, Greece or Canada. And what about products manufactured in 3 or 4 different places? Will a product made by Siemens in India or Turkey be deemed inferior to a similar product made in a German Siemens plant?

All this means that traditional, deep-rooted and often misleading stereotypes can hold countries back. Brazil – a country associated with carnival, samba, tropical fruit, tourism, football and financial instability – is the world's eighth largest economy. It designed the British Royal Air Force primary trainer, the Tucano, and in a good year makes as many cars as Britain. So Brazil needs an image which allows its industrial potential to be treated with the same respect as its ability to give tourists a good time.

Finally there's tourism – the world's fourth largest industry, growing at 9% per year. Some countries depend largely on tourism for their earnings and have developed a sophisticated tourist infrastructure. Some of the most unlikely countries are highly reliant on it. New Zealand's largest foreign exchange earner is tourism. The danger for countries which rely heavily on traditional tourism is that sun, sea and sand is in danger of becoming a commodity driven by fierce competition on price, attracting more and more people who usually spend less and less money individually. If Morocco can sell it for 100, and the Gambia may sell it for 90, Portugal certainly won't want to sell it for 85. The alternative is for countries to trade-up, differentiating themselves like consumer brands – emphasising their art, culture, food, architecture, landscape and other unique characteristics through sophisticated imagery.

So tourism joins export and inward investment in the commercial battle between nations, fought using modern marketing tools. And the images that a nation has in tourism, inward investment and brand export inevitably overlap and coalesce. Success will depend on handling this in a sophisticated and co-ordinated fashion so that a complex nation like Brazil has a clear, attractive and differentiated image which meets its needs for tourism, export and inward investment and so contributes to commercial success. This is why increasing numbers of nations are adopting the marketing techniques that companies have been using for years.

4. Branding a modern nation: successes and failures

When countries change, it can take quite a long time for damaging, left-over stereotypes to disappear. Branding works when it projects and reinforces a changing reality – but it can be counter-productive if it isn't rooted in fact.

The New Spain

Spain, once a world power of the first rank, went into a long, self-destructive decline culminating in a hideous civil war. It degenerated into an isolated, autarkic, poverty-stricken, authoritarian anachronism, hardly part of modern Europe at all. Since Franco's death in 1975, it has transformed itself into a modern, well-off, European democracy. The reality has changed but so has the image. Spain has carefully orchestrated and promoted its re-entry into the European family.

The Joan Miro sun symbol was an identifier for a massive promotional programme closely linked to national change and modernisation. Institutional and tourist advertising on a national and regional level, the creation of successful international business schools, the growth, privatisation and globalisation of Spanish multinationals like Repsol, Telefonica and Union Fenosa, the rebuilding and beautifying of major cities like Barcelona and Bilbao, the self-mocking, sexually explicit tragicomic films of

Almodovar and his contemporaries, political devolution, the Barcelona Olympics and the Seville International Exhibition of 1992 all underline and exemplify the change.

This programme of activities, a proportion of it carefully planned and co-ordinated, but much based around individual and corporate initiative, has rehabilitated and revitalised Spain both in its own eyes and in the eyes of the world. Spain is among the best examples of modern, successful national branding because it keeps on building on what truly exists; it incorporates, absorbs, and embraces a wide variety of activities to form and project a loose and multi-faceted yet coherent, interlocking, mutually supportive whole. Its coherence and ubiquity are similar to that of the British and French 19th century imperial projects – though its goals are very different.

An Australian Republic?

Australia has moved significantly away from its historic British Commonwealth 'White Australia' roots – increased immigration from Asian countries is associated with much closer trade and diplomatic relations in the Asia-Pacific. Australian culture is no longer dominated by Britain and the United States. Australian cities are full of restaurants from Indonesia, Thailand and Japan. Melbourne has the world's largest population of Greeks after Athens. Aboriginal Australians win major art prizes. As the demographic, diplomatic and commercial balance has changed, the imagery of Australia has been carefully modulated, but the national symbolism has changed less than might be expected. Coins still carry the Queen's head and many other symbolic totems are still in place. This helps to explain why Australia is so torn about becoming a republic. While it may seem an obvious and sensible thing to do, reflecting the new reality of Australia as an integral part of the Asia-Pacific world, it also means cutting loose from the last symbolic link with much of the nation's history. The visual changes demanded for this last step, a new flag and so on, would mark a new era just as they did in 1789 in France.

A Reality Check

Many other nations have found that active steps to develop a new image in the world are necessary because a changing reality is leaving perceptions far behind. Ireland and Portugal have long been perceived as marginal and somewhat backward. But Ireland today, the 'Celtic Tiger', is far from a poverty-stricken, depopulated, priest-ridden bog, nor is Portugal a country which makes most of its living exporting cleaning ladies and taxi drivers. With their high growth rates and ability to attract technologically-sophisticated inward investment, both have been involved, at least to some extent, in image change programmes which emphasise and capitalise on the changes that have taken place in the last two decades of the 20th century.

These success stories stem from a new image to reflect, project and reinforce a changed reality. But the example of Malaysia shows how it can be injudicious to draw attention to yourself. In the first half of 1999 Malaysia launched an advertising campaign in *The Economist* and other major publications charting its recovery from near economic collapse. But this campaign coincided with scandalous political upheavals, descending into courtroom farce. Accusations of sodomy, flagrant police violence, even the literal exposure of dirty linen in the trial of the former deputy Prime Minister and heir-apparent, have highlighted serious questions about political freedom within Malaysian society.

The lesson is that Malaysia would be better off keeping a low profile until it sorts out some of its grosser follies.

Rebranding Britain

But the most high-profile and controversial identity programme of recent years is Tony Blair's crusade to 'rebrand Britain'. So is it working?

Because both the media and the public immediately recognised it as a profile-changing operation, it was an easy target to attack. But in reality, the government's project is serious and important.

The image of Britain in many parts of the world remains dominated by what seem to us comically outdated stereotypes – stiff upper lips, Dimple Haig whisky, Sherlock Holmes and other dusty symbols of an imperial past long-forgotten by most Britons. Mark Leonard's study *Britain™: Renewing our identity*, published by the think-tank Demos, and the *Made in Britain* study by Wolff Olins confirmed that newer equally out-of-date stereotypes of Britain as strike-prone, old-fashioned and out of touch also remain strong. But these 1970s images are no more accurate or helpful than those of the 1950s or 1900s to British companies competing in a global market. The Demos report quotes David Mercer, Head of Design at BT:

"British Telecom did research into the appropriateness of the name British Telecom in overseas markets. We found that we had problems with the name in certain parts of the world – Japan was a particular problem – where the name "British" was understood to stand for "of the past", "colonial", not about innovation, not about high technology, or the future or moving forward. Given the fact that we are in a fast-moving, highly innovative, creative area in telecommunications, the name British was a problem, and that was why we changed from British Telecom to BT."

Misunderstandings and misconceptions about Britain still persist. Anyone who travels abroad knows how little Britain is reported in the world's media – and how even this coverage is dominated by insubstantial gossip about the less significant members of the Royal Family. Britain surely cannot remain the home of the global soap, stuck with imagery which may lead British companies to think that the only sensible thing to do with their British identity is to ditch it. Global competitiveness can be built from positive national associations, but negative connotations just get in the way of doing business.

The Blair government emphasises Britain's new service industries, especially its creative businesses, to highlight its vitality, its openness and its multicultural society and, above all, to open the eyes of potential customers to some of Britain's strengths – to what Britain has to sell in an increasingly knowledge-driven world. The central message is that Britain's reality has changed dramatically and that its image must be transformed to reflect this. British multiculturalism and diversity are not just an irreversible fact but a potentially invaluable asset. So 'Rebranding Britain' is a serious, important contribution to improving and correcting Britain's image – socially, culturally and commercially – in the world.

These changes don't happen quickly, they are incremental not dramatic. If the current momentum is sustained, Britain's image in the world will change. It takes time and much serious work to track and quantify this, but anecdotal evidence and coverage in the global media suggests that the Blair government's moves have already had some impact.

This government's overt embrace of marketing techniques, the national annual report, the attention paid to the now notorious focus groups, the symbols of change like the Millennium Dome all point to a government which is determined to move a hesitant, and perhaps instinctively unwilling, nation to project a clear, contemporary, accurate picture of itself. Whatever the reaction in Britain, Blair's initiatives on branding are being very closely scrutinised by a number of other European countries which face related issues.

5. Putting the unknown nation on the map

Countries which have thought most about branding issues have been those, like Britain, with some kind of traditional position, influence and reputation which they seek to change or improve.

But, paradoxically, it is those who have yet to start who need branding most. The most urgent problems are faced by small new nations which nobody knows. In fact, most countries are small and little known except by their immediate neighbours. Of the 180 or so nations in the world, only about 50 have populations of more than 10 million. Many have a broken, interrupted or chaotic history, others are very new and often not at all clear what it is they have to shout about. These are the nations who most need to develop and then project a clear identity which can differentiate them from the competition.

Take a country like the Ukraine. In principle, it could have quite a lot of advantages. It is big, twice the size of France; it has 50 million people and is a nuclear power with significant mineral and agricultural resources and even an attractive coastline. In the 19th century, as part of Tsarist Russia, the Ukraine was a significant exporter of high-quality agricultural products and its Crimean coast was a popular holiday destination. But, today, exhortations about investing or holidaying in the Ukraine have rather a hollow ring. Of course, this is partly because the Ukraine's facilities are not up to an acceptable world standard. But, if the reality is wretched, the image is even worse. The only Ukranian product anybody can remember is the nuclear fall-out from Chernobyl. So while the Ukraine could become a country on the global company's investment horizon, with the resources and the potential for development, it needs to work out how to fulfil it. The issue for the Ukraine is when the brand-building should begin. If the appalling perception is an accurate reflection of reality, it may be safer not to start now. But if the economy won't improve unless there's investment, and investment depends on self-promotion, it may be necessary to get going quickly. In that case, the key is not to tell lies and pretend things are better than they really are.

And how many people – apart from real specialists – can tell the five former Soviet Central Asian 'stans' apart? In reality, Uzbekistan, Kyrgyzstan, Turkmenistan, Kazakhstan and Tajikistan are very different. Some are large, some small, some have huge resources, others don't, some are old-style communist dictatorships, others are evolving in a more or less democratic direction and, of course, they all dislike each other. But they've got a real problem in establishing who and what they are in a world increasingly cluttered with 'new' nations. Very few new countries have established a clear brand, let alone a positive one where they are known for something other than war.

Countries with a chaotic, wretched or turbulent past which are attempting to emerge with a new social, political, industrial, commercial and cultural persona must eventually realise that in order to be noticed in the world at large, and to be assisted in the process of change, rather than lumped together as a bunch of corrupt, useless self-destructive basket-cases, they too will have to take active steps to create a positive identity. Inevitably for these countries such identities must be based more around opportunities for the future than today's reality. In this sort of situation an identity programme can act as a catalyst for change. If they don't launch such programmes it will be increasingly difficult to attract assistance. It will be increasingly difficult for them to help themselves and they will remain trapped in a morass.

What these countries have not yet realised is that they can adopt similar branding strategies to those which have been attempted elsewhere – usually by much better-known and better-off countries. There are of course a lot of potential pitfalls – but the basic techniques and approaches are similar. It is only a matter of time before they and virtually every other nation put brand-building on their agendas.

6. How to brand a country: a seven-step plan

The process of brand-building has already begun in some of the more forward-looking countries. Once it takes off it will become unstoppable. The issue is no longer whether it matters, but how to do it successfully and effectively. Managing an identity programme for a nation in the twenty-first century is going to demand political, managerial and technical skills. If it is too overt, it will be seen as shrill, authoritarian and therefore unpalatable in a citizens' democracy. If it is too implicit it simply won't be seen or heard at all. It cannot be conjured up out of thin air – it must draw from reality but it has to be focussed, recognisable, coherent and attractive. The most successful identities are not invented, they are based upon a mood, upon things which are actually happening, which they encapsulate visually and then promote.

There are seven basic stages in brand-building and many pitfalls to avoid. A government planning to launch an identity programme should:

(1) Set up a working party with representatives of government, industry, the arts, education and the media to start the programme.

(2) Find out how the nation is perceived both by its own people and by nations abroad through quantitative and qualitative

research. It's a great mistake to assume that outsiders know very much, or anything at all for that matter, about your own country. In London, I was once shown a map of Europe by a Taiwanese official in which there was no British Isles.

(3) Develop a process of consultation with opinion-leaders to look at national strengths and weaknesses, and compare them with the results of the internal and external studies.

(4) Create the central idea on which the strategy is based with professional advisors. This needs to be a powerful simple idea, which captures the unique qualities of the nation and can be used as a base from which the entire programme can be developed. The best way to do this is to prepare a page, then a paragraph, then a phrase, which may then become the dreaded strapline.

(5) Develop ways of articulating the central idea visually. Designers should not just look at logos and tourist ad displays, but everything from the design of airports where visitors arrive to the embassies that represent the nation abroad.

(6) Look at how the messages required for tourism, inward investment and export can be co-ordinated and modulated so that they are appropriate for each audience.

(7) Create a liaison system through the working party to launch and sustain the programme in government activities and to encourage supportive action from appropriate organisations in commerce, industry, the arts, media and so on.

The project should then be rolled out gradually without making a big song and dance. This means looking at every opportunity. Not just the obvious tradefairs, advertising, and commercial work in embassies; but the look and reception that people get in airports, stations, government buildings, broadcasting, even restaurants.

Everywhere, in fact, that can contribute to the idea of a country. It's worth remembering that people are influenced by all they see, feel and eat as much as by what they read or hear. That's why film festivals are quite as significant as commercial missions.

While a national branding plan is more complex and involves more coordination than a commercial identity programme, the essentials are the same. Both commercial and national brand-building are concerned with the creation of clear, simple, differentiating propositions often built around emotional qualities expressing some kind of superiority, which can be readily symbolised both verbally and visually. These propositions must be easy to understand and sufficiently flexible to operate in a wide variety of situations with a large number of audiences.

Governments can create the mood and lead and co-ordinate the new image. Coherent efforts within every department – culture, arts, sport, industry, education, transport and environment and, of course, foreign affairs can stimulate, inspire and steer. There has to be a powerful visual focus, an agreement to make it work and an adequate power base and funding.

The key is to get a clear idea, make it manifest by visualising it and implementing it on all those official and influential activities where it is possible and credible and in this way to create or co-ordinate a movement which influential organisations and individuals outside government circles join because it suits them. The example of Spain is significant. Adolfo Dominguez, clothes designer, Pedro Almodovar, film-maker, and Santiago Calatrava, architect and engineer, are not government hacks hired by the hour. They are world-class figures whose work shares the courage and optimism of the new Spain, partly at any rate because over many years, the Spanish Government in the centre and the regions worked hard at creating and projecting a courageous and optimistic vision, based on a reality of change, which inspired them and in which they shared.

In countries with an authoritarian tradition there could well be a tendency to impose solutions from above – and to coerce or at least put pressure on non-governmental institutions to follow the agreed policy. This would be counterproductive. We don't want any 21st-century Leni Reifenstahls. The essence of such programmes is that they capture a mood, and individuals and organisations sense this and join in voluntarily. Compulsion doesn't work because the identity will emerge through a multiplicity of messages, and not just a few single great events – although there isn't any harm in a Millennium Dome. All countries communicate all the time. They send out millions of messages everyday through political action or inaction, through popular culture, through products, services, behaviour, arts and architecture. Collectively, all these millions of messages represent an idea of what the nation as a whole is up to, what it feels, what it wants, what it believes in. It should be the task of government – with a very light touch – to set the tone for these messages, and to lead by example where appropriate so that something credible, coherent and realistic can emerge.

Within a few years, identity management will be seen as a perfectly normal manifestation of what is now called joined-up government. A successful brand will be seen as a key national asset. No country will be able to ignore the way the rest of the world sees it. Politicians everywhere in the world now realise that every nation has an identity – they can either seek to manage it or it will manage them.

Part Two:
Companies
The global rise of the corporate state?

Companies which do business across national boundaries are nothing new. The East India Company was founded in 1599. It did virtually all of its business in India but the idea that it should somehow 'adapt' to India never remotely crossed its mind. A somewhat later company, Citroën the French automotive company was intensely ambitious for global success. The company which established its first plant in Paris in 1919 had factories in Belgium, Italy, Britain and Germany and was exporting to more than 60 territories within 10 years. But it remained profoundly French, in management style, product, culture – everything.

Nationality was until quite recently linked with economic and political power. In the heyday of the British East India Company you couldn't tell where the company ended and British political influence began. In the 20th century, Rolls-Royce, Sony and Fiat derived their reputation, their perceived personality and quite a lot of their sales from their national origins. These companies were not exceptions, they were the rule. Most companies have always derived their culture, behaviour patterns and most of their senior people from a single homeland on whose stock exchange their shares were usually quoted.

Today, however, companies are not simply much bigger than ever before as they race to merge across borders, they are also trying to become more culturally adaptable. They want to operate and to be at home everywhere. Being effective across a wide range of cultures inevitably means toning down or even eliminating the company's own national roots and affiliations.

The process of aggrandisement also involves companies in issues which they have never previously encountered. Most global companies despite repetitive and tiresome muttering of the mantra 'Think Global – Act Local' remain uncomfortable and ill-at-ease outside their home territories. They need to develop a clear identity and ethos which is not linked to their national origins. But they also need to get more involved with their host communities. Companies know they have more power, new responsibilities and therefore more interface with society. When companies are running many of the things that used to be in the public sector – planes, trains, public utilities, even prisons and schools – the public has started to ask the same questions of companies that politicians are used to facing. The horrific rail accident at Paddington in October 1999 raised immediate questions about the balance between profit and safety. The old relatively well-defined relationships between the corporate world and the rest of society have broken down, and it is not yet clear where the new boundaries will be drawn.

And while the nation-state sometimes feels threatened by corporate power, many global companies feel bewildered, beleaguered and misunderstood by the public. In order to cope with its new vast size and the complexities which derive from it, the global company is taking on many of the tasks, characteristics and burdens of the traditional nation-state, even of 19th-century empire. So far it has not been doing this consciously, but in a sporadic, uncoordinated and, it has to be said, not very successful fashion. But some of the similarities are uncanny – and companies are increasingly becoming conscious of how much they can learn from countries. As they learn to use nation-building techniques in order to gain popular legitimacy, businessmen move into areas of activity which, as yet, they barely comprehend, but which are very familiar to the politicians who run countries.

7. From national champions to corporate patriotism

Until recently global companies all had a national root. They may have called themselves global or trans-national, or international or even multi-local, but in the end they all had a home base which was rooted in one or very occasionally two countries. In other words, to use my colleague Brian Boylan's phrase, they were always 'global from somewhere'. Now though they are going to learn to be just global – or if you prefer 'global from everywhere'.

Although many industries – financial services, life sciences, automobiles – are changing and globalising, it is the telecoms industry which embodies all of these changes most dramatically. Only a few years ago the telecoms business was sleeping quietly, with each company ignoring and ignored by the rest of the world. National utilities, mostly state-owned operated in a stagnant backwater. Today telecoms is going through a period of dramatic technological change, of convergence between satellite, cable and computers and necessarily of dramatic globalisation. Telecoms businesses, once made up of national champions representing the fixed-link telephone business in each country, are now seeking to shed old names, identities, cultures, technologies, behaviour patterns, everything else you can think of, as they become global infocoms players.

It is not just global companies from a single industry merging, industrial convergence is creating entirely new players made up of many industries – as information technology, broadcasting and telecommunications become one huge industry. The mergers, alliances and partnerships are so complex and so rapid, that it is almost impossible for any non-specialist to follow them. The issue of identity has become increasingly significant because nobody, including the telecoms companies themselves, is quite sure what countries and what business they're in anymore. That is why the national players are beginning to shed their traditional names and identities. British Telecom was one of the first, it became BT, Finnish Telecom became Senora. Even Deutsche Telekom calls itself plain Telekom. Senora (formerly part of the Finnish PTT) is involved with the Baltic republics, with Russia, with Lebanon and Turkey amongst others. Through Turkey it's involved with some former Soviet republics in Central Asia. In most of these situations it has alliances and partnerships with other companies. Senora is still quoted only on the Finnish stock exchange, and it's still run by Finns. But for how long?

These identity issues are especially acute when mergers bring together two organisations with equally strong but wholly incompatible identities, on which their individual success have been based.

Look at Daimler-Chrysler. In the deal between Daimler Benz and Chrysler, two national icons have come together. Chrysler's Jeep trades on open spaces, the rugged American way and by implication freedom, liberty and democracy. Its appearance – powerful, coarse, simple and big – is archetypally American. Mercedes-Benz on the other hand is iconically Teutonic, the best, most precise, understated, efficient engineering that money can buy. These two companies and their products have been more than traditional national flag-carriers; in some ways they have both shaped and been shaped by perceptions of their respective nations.

But what is the new Daimler-Chrysler? It isn't German anymore, nor is it American. This isn't just an issue of nationality – it's about the way people inside the company do things, what customers expect and what products stand for. It is about identity. What are dealers, employers and customers supposed to feel about the products of Daimler-Chrysler? Will the Jeep and the Mercedes M-Class be produced on the same line to the same quality? Will the Jeep eventually get a Mercedes star? Will Chrysler dealers expect Mercedes margins? Will Chrysler customers expect Mercedes (i.e. German) quality and levels of service? Will Mercedes customers worry about lower (i.e. American) standards of quality? Whose research and development systems, whose production methods, whose distribution patterns will come out on top? What about titles, hierarchy, rates of pay and other symbols of internal status?

More important than any of these, but ultimately bound up with each of them, what will the new combined company stand for? It cannot continue to represent two nations, it will have to create an entirely new idea about itself which its people everywhere in the world will have to understand and live by. It cannot be global from somewhere, because apart from anything else, it's quite conceivable that Daimler-Chrysler will in the course of time expand again. It might take over a Japanese or Korean automotive company, which will bring with it another set of national/cultural issues.

Conflicts of interest

Though politicians continue to promote national business through embassies and trade missions abroad, the idea that "What's good for General Motors is good for America" – that companies' and countries' interests always coincide – is being rapidly eroded. In some industries, notably aerospace and defence, it is still difficult to untangle where politics ends and business begins.

But as companies continue to merge across national boundaries, as their focus and activities become more global, they begin to develop a broader perspective. They compare one country with another in terms of taxation, employment conditions, quality of labour force, wage rates and so on. The interests of the company and of any one particular nation begin to diverge, even conflict.

Where to invest for instance? Jaguar and Rover are no longer

British-owned, even though they remain national icons. Both Ford, the U.S-owner of Jaguar and BMW the German proprietor of Rover had to be bribed with considerable financial subsidies by the British government (intending, of course, to protect employment) in order to expand (maybe even retain) production sites of these two classic English brands in Britain. BMW even threatened to take Rover to Hungary.

Where to put head offices and how to reduce tax? Increasingly global companies with global interests are moving away from their traditional home bases to places where it is easier to do business. Swedish Perstorp now runs its global flooring business from London. Like a number of other Swedish companies, Perstorp finds that London is easier for communication, the tax burden is lighter and its people find it an attractive place to live. Meanwhile some British road haulage companies are threatening to re-register their vehicles outside the UK under 'flags of convenience' where their tax burden will be reduced. These are just two examples among many. For global companies national frontiers look increasingly petty and artificial. Increasingly, they put national sentiment on one side and base themselves and their activities where it suits them best.

Developing a shared ethos

In these new global companies with two or more national roots, the key is to find a binding central idea which everyone can embrace and then symbolise it powerfully, verbally and visually. As we have seen, this cannot be related to national identity.

Traditionally, vast complex global companies have spent a lot of time building brands for external consumption but relatively little time seriously building up their identities for their own staff and other stakeholders. Nation-building in the 19th century started in primary schools and was continued during compulsory military service. Of course, global companies can't capture their employees so young. Nevertheless they are having a go at indoctrination. In

1998/99 as part of a major programme of corporate integration, the newly formed Daimler-Chrysler organisation launched a series of advertisements in leading business magazines underlining the commitment of all their people to the new enterprise and featuring individual employees at all levels of the organisation in Germany and the US who, not unsurprisingly, shared the same can-do attitudes towards the new venture. Although these advertisements appeared in business magazines purporting to be for public consumption, they were aimed, primarily at any rate, towards insiders of the new organisation and its dealers. It is unclear, at least to me, whether apart from the standard verbiage about commitment, quality and passion for service, Daimler-Chrysler has discovered or invented any binding central idea for the new enterprise. What is clear, though, is that the company recognises that it has to make a huge effort to create a new identity to embrace both German and American roots. This is just a small example of the enormous efforts global companies are making to understand and manage the changes taking place inside them and to mutate away from their national roots.

Daimler-Chrysler is still largely a product-based manufacturing business. But identity is an even more significant issue in a global service business, like Holiday Inn, Burger King or American Express where service should be seamless and consistent everywhere in the world. Persuading staff in Moscow, Mexico City, Minneapolis and Manchester to offer similar levels of service is not easy. These new global organisations need to develop and project an ethos powerful enough to get their own people to work effectively together and to represent the same corporate idea wherever in the world they are.

Major airlines are of course quintessential global service businesses. Historically almost all airlines grew up as national flag carriers. Lufthansa was Teutonic efficiency; Alitalia, a bizarre mixture of Michaelangelo, Benetton, Verdi and pasta and so it went on. Today these national stereotypes get in the way of global business. Hence the attempt by British Airways to present a new global personality. The old British Airways identity was built around a caricatured English reserve, polite, efficient, cool – a kind of 'anyone for tennis' style. But because British Airways made alliances or took over French, German, Australian and other airlines, it found that a large proportion of both its staff and passengers no longer originated in Britain. It seemed perfectly sensible to modulate the appearance and behaviour of the airline to line up with its commercial reality. And that's how and why the new global identity of BA was created.

BA replaced its British identity and chose to focus on ethnic and national identities from different parts of the world. In retrospect one can see that it might have been wiser to eschew the idea of nationality entirely. However it's easy to be wise after the event. It's not particularly surprising that this early attempt at introducing a global identity has not quite worked; it's actually much more surprising that many more disasters haven't yet happened amongst newly globalising companies who are struggling to find out who and what they are.

In their different ways BA, with its new identity, and Daimler-Chrysler with its advertising are pioneers, struggling to create coherence, cohesion and a sense of unity in their widely dispersed multi-cultural organisations. Big companies increasingly find that their national roots get in the way of their global growth.

The brand: a new focus for loyalty

This is where brands come in. BA is both a corporation and a brand, but Daimler-Chrysler certainly isn't, because the different brands have become separated from the corporation's identity.

The power of brands for consumers is well known – though sometimes even identity consultants are surprised by it. There was recently a bizarre story in *The Sunday Times* under the headline, "What the well dressed killer is wearing". "For terrorists of the world" the piece claimed "only global brand names will do". A long-serving police officer was quoted "Many of these people now think they are something special. Designer clothing is seen as a statement of their position giving them street cred".

Evidently brands have come a long way since their origins as mundane household products; jam or cornflakes in a grocer's shop. Today brands are highly visible objects of consumption which have become a significant focus for the individual's loyalties. Global brands, some mass market like Nike, Coca-Cola, Burger King, others expensive like Prada, Gucci and Hermes demonstrate the individual's need for self-definition. These global brands also provide the comfort of representing an idea – youth, energy, good taste, money and so on. Individuals from every nation seem to be susceptible to this extraordinary phenomenon. While brand loyalty is no substitute for nationality it certainly complements it.

The issue for the corporation is whether it can and should attempt to transfer loyalty from the brands it markets to itself as an organisation. If like Unilever, P&G or Diageo it owns a lot of well-known brands but is little-known itself this will be difficult, but if like Orange or Manchester United the brand is also the company then this doesn't represent such a problem. Virgin is so far the clearest expression of the corporation as a brand. It's not what Virgin does that matters so much as how it does it. Virgin doesn't market products and services. It markets an idea of itself, laid back, alternative, challenging the fat cats. But to sustain high levels of loyalty the brand needs also to sustain high and consistent levels of performance in absolutely everything it does, and that, as Virgin knows to its cost, is not easy.

The argument for the corporation directly to associate itself with its more attractive, better-known and more powerful brands is very persuasive. And although the risks are high, so are the rewards. It's likely that it will happen increasingly. As this happens it will create an increasing incentive for the corporation to adopt a consistent, sympathetic and credible public position.

8. The ethics of business: why global companies are public property

But global companies don't just need to recreate their identities. They have to deal with very different expectations from society as well. Executives running companies today started their careers in much simpler times. Governments set the rules and businesses obeyed them. Companies did not think about their ethical responsibilities or the public consequences of what they did. They were simply expected to make the best possible profit for their shareholders. Even though the familiar cliché of 'shareholder value' is still ritually trotted out for the sake of financial analysts, most managements now know that blindly focussing on profitability to the exclusion of everything else will prove self-defeating. The days when management could claim that the only social responsibility of business was to make a profit, thereby producing wealth, are now coming rapidly to a not so peaceful end.

In the last two decades, global companies, rather to their surprise and frequently to their embarrassment, have become front-page news – not just when they open new plants or lay off workers, but because their activities are now scrutinised like those of governments. What companies get up to, and how they behave is now a matter of major concern. And what grabs headlines is bad news.

Global corporations are still for the most part slow, clumsy and defensive when they deal with the media. But it is not just 'spin' that businessmen could learn from politicians. The main reason that companies are so bad at dealing with issues involving the public interest is that they have only just begun to think through the public consequences of their behaviour and actions. And while big business seems to sense that the rules have changed, it doesn't know yet what the new rules are.

A better educated, less deferential public and an aggressive media, combined with shifts in technology, mean that the law is now lagging behind public opinion. The public is demanding that companies do more than just follow the rules. Just look at the row over genetically modified foods. Public opinion is taking the lead and government and business are hesitantly following. And globalisation means that these issues are multiplied manifold – because the legal systems in many developing countries don't guarantee what western publics expect as basic standards on employment conditions, child labour and the environment. What's more the globalisation of the media means that companies have nowhere to hide.

This shift in public attitude comes from the realisation that companies exercise real political power. The privatisation of telecoms, health, transport and so on has made companies central to our everyday lives. And globally, companies increasingly have the ability to shop around between countries for the best deal in terms of business conditions, taxes and regulations when deciding where to produce or invest. This means that they are often perceived to be in the driving seat in their relationships with national governments, because we don't have global regulatory standards – yet.

So people, consumer groups, environmental groups, and the media demand that power is combined with responsibility, and scrutinise companies as never before. Companies react by attempting to legitimise themselves – to become a respected part of the fabric of society. They are just beginning to comprehend the immense scale of their social responsibility. Legitimising yourself is not just about obeying the law – it is about anticipating it, policing yourself and your suppliers, and being ready to justify your activities in terms of their overall social impact. The extent to which these lessons have been learned is uneven and varies from one company, one industry, and even one country to another, but it is certainly happening.

Take outsourcing. Because of competitive pressure, companies have looked for the cheapest place they can to produce goods at the quality they want. But Nike and its competitors never dreamed that it was up to them to see that their suppliers in the developing world didn't use child labour. It was something they never even thought about. Well now they know better. Even third party suppliers have to be carefully supervised and regarded as part of the corporate family; if they aren't, they may behave in a way which will shame and humiliate their global partners. Low wages, child labour, backbreaking working conditions, the global company gets the blame from investigative journalists feeding on drama and exposure. This is a story that keeps on running. *The Sunday Times* of 26 September 1999 offers a fairly typical global companies shock story – "Top Shops use Europe's Gulag Labour" – "Marks & Spencer, C&A, Debenhams and Laura Ashley are among companies using factories where workers are fainting at their machines". And that's just for starters. This is why so many companies are getting 'ethical' and signing up to codes of conduct.

But having a new ethical approach is not always enough. Companies also need to win the public trust, and to persuade people that they are sincere. This is borne out by Europe's current ill-informed, emotionally-charged and very noisy debate about genetically modified foods where Big Business, personified by Monsanto, is cast in the role of villain. Monsanto is permanently on the back foot because the public is – legitimately – sceptical of the standards and behaviour of many big players in the food and agri-chemical industry, and these companies have often found themselves struggling to think about questions of values and public trust. There is a need to have a well-informed debate about the GM issue, but if it happens it won't bear much resemblance to the one which is going on at the moment. It is evident that

Monsanto in particular and global companies in general, despite their superficial sophistication in public relations matters, are handing this business badly. Despite all of the lessons from PR companies about 'crisis management' business doesn't really know how to deal with public criticism. Business people could and will learn a lot from politicians, whose public life is one long effort to manage unexpected events.

If pressure from lobbies, the media and intermittently and dramatically from consumers isn't enough there's also employee pressure which drives the corporation into legitimising itself. Global companies are competing in a knowledge-driven economy for the highest-skilled and the best employees. And these people are not just looking for the best salaries, but good employment conditions and a company whose ethos and values they can believe in.

We can see the impact which employee pressure can have in one of the highest-profile corporate change programmes of recent years – that of Shell. As an Anglo-Dutch company which operates around the world, Shell has much more experience in operating across cultures than most other global companies. Yet it has still managed to make large and costly mistakes, which badly damaged its reputation, especially over its dealings in Nigeria. The Brent Spar episode was also damaging, even if the focus was later as much on Greenpeace's claims after their initial publicity coup. While the media and non-governmental pressure was intense, and the share price fell, Shell executives have said that the factor which did most to influence the change of direction and ethos was pressure from its own employees. They had become ashamed to admit that they worked for Shell at dinner parties or in the pub.

This explains why Shell has tried to create a new mission which its employees are comfortable with. Shell is embarking on a major process of social and environmental reporting, informal consultation mechanisms with its staff and a new appraisal system intended to make community, social or environmental work a valued part of job performance. Shell's internal changes, regarded with some scepticism by its more traditional managers, were accompanied by a campaign in British newspapers which explained this rather belated conversion to environmental issues. The Shell Report of 1998 *Profits and Principles: does there have to be a choice?* encapsulated the global company's attempt to talk soft, to emphasise its sense of responsibility to society as a whole and its new willingness to listen – 'Tell Shell'.

This stuff from Shell and others is not the result of the milk of human kindness suddenly flowing. It's an acknowledgement of the fact that, other things being equal, people buy products and services from the companies they know best and like best. Shell knows that if it can persuade you and me that it cares more about the environment than its competitors – not necessarily such a tall order if you look at the record of most of them – then we might decide to buy our petrol from them. In other words legitimisation can bring respectability, even affection, which brings loyalty, which brings turnover, which brings greater profits, which brings, wait for it, 'shareholder value'.

But it's important not to exaggerate the impact of all this on corporate life and the corporate management style. In my experience there are very few large corporations, even the most intelligent and far-sighted who regard the issues which I have just examined as their highest priority. For the global corporation the core issues remain how to grow, beat the competition and make sense of changes that are taking place around them. And by changes they usually mean technological changes, the impact of the internet and so on. They are taking longer to realise that linked to these issues of technological change are the issues debated in this pamphlet – social change, cultural change, relationships with stakeholders. All substantial issues, but not yet quite at the heart of most management's concerns.

Many global companies, of course, appreciate that acting responsibly to all their stakeholders may involve an attempt to reconcile conflicting interests – more profits on the one hand; more social and environmental management and expenditure on the other. A few companies feel that enlightened self-interest is at the heart of it. If you behave well, people will buy your products.

The attempt to recognise and then reconcile these conflicting interests will be at the heart of many boardroom battles over the next few years.

9. Is the corporation becoming a state?

So new pressures on global companies and their relationships with their stakeholders, from suppliers to customers and staff, seem to be driving them into ever greater public activity. This offers both an opportunity to expand, grow and make profits, and to gain the respect and admiration of the society upon whose goodwill the corporation depends.

Despite the criticisms and their evident inexperience, their size, power and ambition drives global companies into activities which have traditionally been the preserve of the state. There are plenty of global companies which operate inside nation-states where the state provides minimal or no facilities for health, education or even security. Extraction companies have little choice about where they operate, they must go to where the oil or minerals are. Inside the borders of Angola, Colombia and similar rugged places, companies have to police their own territory with their own military whom they call 'security'. They have to create health, education and similar facilities. Sometimes they look like states inside states. *The Guardian* compared Shell's healthcare provision facilities in Nigeria with those of the Nigerian government.

Tata, India's largest company operating in hotels, steel, trucks, electronics and a hundred other things has always provided much more for its employees than the nation ever could: its steel town at

Jamshedpur in the corrupt and poverty-stricken state of Bihar has been an admired model in a sea of anarchy for years. Tata, although unusual at the moment, is not alone.

Getting involved in the welfare of very poor people may be familiar to Shell, but it has come as a bit of a shock to Nike and for that matter Marks & Spencer and Debenhams. But global companies learn fast. We can reasonably assume that within a very short time global companies will develop all the facilities required in health, education, security and welfare to manage their empires effectively. And what's more they will take advantage of all the opportunities available to them to indoctrinate their suppliers, employees and other so called stakeholders with their own corporate philosophy.

So companies are winning the loyalty of their staff by providing them with welfare, training and other services, much as countries did in the late 19th- and early 20th-centuries. But companies are also finding themselves taking on some of the international roles that countries have developed.

In previous centuries, countries invented foreign and diplomatic services. As their relationships moved beyond simple issues of war and peace to a complex mesh of commercial, cultural and diplomatic activity, they opened up networks of offices – called embassies – all around the world.

This was a strategy not just to exercise but also to legitimate power. In fact, embassies played three important roles. They gave countries a voice in another country – so that they could more effectively use their influence to lobby the host government for the policies they wanted. They also provided eyes and ears with which to gather valuable intelligence. And having this presence abroad also provided for accountability – creating an opportunity for local interests to get their point of view across to you, thereby increasing your involvement with that society and legitimising the power and influence which you exercised. The goals of global companies today are very similar.

This is why companies increasingly handle their affairs themselves. It's evident that Shell knows more about Nigeria, and BP more about Colombia where they have investments and facilities than most nation-states which have embassies in these territories. What's more these major multinationals don't rely on embassies of national governments to negotiate on their behalf – they do it themselves. They have a lot to gain – and to lose – and they know what they are talking about. Similarly in Beijing, Delhi and similar cities, global companies have their own embassies and ambassadors. They don't call them that, but the function is identical.

For countries, the creation of a network of embassies also had consequences for the way in which power was exercised at home. The people closest to the situation on the ground, who therefore often had the best information, naturally won a greater say in what the policy was. Power could be dispersed. Again this process is being replicated by companies. As a result of the most important intelligence being dispersed around the world, many countries are becoming more decentralised and networked so that the people closest to the problems, and with the best knowledge of them, have a greater say in the decisions. It has even been suggested by a few people that some corporations are sufficiently engaged by this democratising process that they will consider enfranchising their staff to elect directors. A version of this co-determination *(Mitbestimmung)* principle already exists in some northern European countries. In practice it hasn't proved too effective – and it's unlikely to spread in this form.

This is because, although countries and companies may become more similar, there will remain a number of major and fundamental differences between them. Governments – at least in most countries – get elected, last a few years and get thrown out. Companies don't work like that. Management is, in the end, responsible to shareholders for profit. Managements only get thrown out when the share price suffers, or the company is taken over or when there's some kind of internal coup. This is not set to change although shifts in consumer expectations will mean that moral imperatives and commercial imperatives will often coincide. And companies will genuinely try to listen to their staff and their share-holders, even if it doesn't always come naturally.

But what we are seeing is a clear shift to less hierarchical and more responsive organisations in which employees around the global corporation, because of their skills and knowledge, are gaining greater responsibility and voice. And this is part of the process by which global companies are dispersing their activities around the world and operating everywhere increasingly in the public domain. They are carrying out their own diplomacy, their own public relations, their own education, health and welfare activities and seeking to present these in the most agreeable light to their various publics. They are realising the importance of positioning themselves in the public arena – because, like nation-states, they are becoming public property.

10. Conclusion: The world in 2050: will we be able to tell countries and companies apart?

When, on the one hand, a nation like Scotland launches itself as a brand and, on the other, health-care and education increasingly slide into the private sector, it seems reasonable for citizens to ask what's going on.

It's clear that in order to increase their competitive edge, especially in tourism, inward investment and export, all areas where success can readily be measured, many nations are already using branding techniques to emphasise their individual and distinct characteristics.

While all this is going on, almost all nations are privatising more or less everything. Public utilities everywhere are privatised, airlines are privatised, even policing and prisons are being partially privatised in some countries. Many smaller nations which nationalised hotels, textile factories, breweries and boat yards years ago, when it was fashionable to nationalise everything that moved – and a lot that didn't – are now rushing to get rid of them. Governments all over the world are trying to do less, but trying to do it better. Genuine efforts are being made to measure performance in the civil service itself as well as in schools, hospitals, and other operations in which the state participates. So government is increasingly adopting the language, the methods, the measurements, the skills and even, to some extent, the culture of business.

The nation is also facing the increasing pressure of regionalism from below and federalism from above. So will nations be so squeezed by global economic giants on the one hand and political developments on the other that their influence will so decrease that they will gradually dwindle into insignificance? Certainly not. What really seems to be happening is that nations are quite rapidly mutating so that they can find new ways of managing themselves, devolving costly public services to private organisations over which they retain ultimate influence, and creating multilateral bodies on specialised issues on which they can have a major impact. NATO and the European Union are two significant examples of how this kind of networking enables the nation to retain a lot of power and influence. While they network power and influence on the one hand, they also reinforce power and influence by brand-building. Contrary to the conventional view, nations aren't really losing influence – they are just reshuffling it.

In fact, it is companies which face the biggest questions today. They may be more powerful than ever before, but even the biggest and most experienced are having difficulty in understanding and giving priority to their new roles and their new networks of responsibility.

They are abandoning the national cultures and identities on which their organisations were based and embracing globalism with enthusiasm if not, as yet, much expertise. They are also seizing the opportunities in areas like health, education and security from which the state is retreating to grow bigger and become more profitable. As they become more visible, they are beginning to comprehend that they have to become more socially responsible and much more sophisticated in the way they handle their relationships with all their publics or stakeholders. These stakeholder relationships grow wider, more complex and more interrelated as the corporations themselves get bigger and their profiles become higher. New power and a higher profile means more pressure to behave properly. Not just because it's morally appropriate, but also because it's good for business.

But many companies are struggling to cope because they simply don't yet have the tools to think clearly about ethics and values. This is where their new responsibilities to society combine with the demands of the new global marketplace for ever bigger global companies. In order to hold themselves together, succeed at a global level, and satisfy expectations for social responsibility, companies are increasingly having to think about:

- **Internal identity programmes.** Create a corporate identity which binds global companies together, giving them a coherent, effective internal ethos which can give cohesion and loyalty to a culturally disparate staff in a genuinely multinational company. This ethos will have to provide a guide to behaviour on the ground, so that decentralised employees can act on the corporate vision.

- **Corporate myths.** In order to do this companies will need to develop myths and values – but just like national identities these must reflect the reality. Many corporations are using their brands to do this.

- **Welfare.** Just as nation-states supplied both material benefits, through education and welfare, and security, through the army, and a say over the content of that identity through parliaments and democratic institutions – now companies are having to do this as well – providing not just training and health-care, but also payment in kind, air miles and other corporate currencies, and giving employees a say over what the decisions are.

- **Democracy.** At the moment, companies increasingly track morale, opinions and consult their staff. It is not impossible to think that in time they might increase openness and extend the information they provide, in staff handbooks and policy documents, to create structures which resemble national constitutions – so that staff know how and where decisions are taken, what the timetables are, and how they can have a voice in the process.

- **Multilateralism.** Another characteristic that nations and global companies have in common is an increasing need to network. Through the European Union, Nato and a complex maze of other organisations, nations attempt to carry out tasks collectively, which none of them, not even the very strongest, could implement alone. Global companies are beginning (not consciously I think) to emulate this concept. In airline, telecoms and other global businesses consortia are emerging in which at least for some purposes and for some of the time normally competing organisations work together. In this airline business, both One World in which British Airways and American Airlines are leading players and Star Alliance which Lufthansa, SAS, Thai and a few other airlines have joined are attempts to build strong global networks. Each partner benefits from the geographic strengths and route network of the others, so that customers are offered what is in theory a seamless global system. These networks, like those of nations are sometimes confusing and ramshackle. Nevertheless because no satisfactory alternative seems to be on offer, and because no individual airline can offer as much as the network, they too are growing and show some signs of success. This is front office stuff. But amongst global companies there is much more networking and sharing of facilities and knowledge in the back office; for purchasing, ticketing, account handling and other less glamorous activities. As global companies continue to grow they are bound to look for opportunities where sharing or networking will be useful. All kinds of activities from Air Miles, which is developing into a kind of global currency, to joint arrangements to fund security or private armies in unstable countries become suitable cases for this kind of treatment.

Of course, this is all crystal ball-gazing, and the future will no doubt continue to surprise us. But it seems clear that nations won't disappear and that companies won't take over the world. But their jostling for influence and position, the intensity with which they compete with each other and learn from each other, and the various ways in which they vie for the admiration, respect and loyalty of the individual is going to make life very interesting. Not just for both countries and companies, but for all of us too – as employees, shareholders, partners, customers and citizens.

Also available from The Foreign Policy Centre

THE FOREIGN POLICY CENTRE MISSION STATEMENT

March 3rd 1999; Free, with £1 p+p, or free with any pamphlet.

When foreign policy affects everything in our lives – from the jobs we do to the food we eat – it is too important to be left to diplomats alone. The Mission Statement sets out the new way of thinking about foreign policy which will guide the Centre as it defines a new agenda to create policies which are ethical, inclusive and effective.

'Likely to be controversial with Mandarins and influential with Ministers' **Financial Times**

GLOBALIZATION – KEY CONCEPTS

David Held & Anthony McGrew, David Goldblatt & Jonathan Perraton

April 12th 1999; £4.95, plus £1 p+p.

Globalization is the buzz-word of the age – but how many people understand it? In this much-needed concise and authoritative guide, globalization's leading theorists thrash out what it really means, and argue that we need to rethink politics to keep up with the changing shape of power. Globalization launches the Key Concepts series – holding all of the hidden assumptions behind foreign policy up to the light, and unpacking the key terms to find out what they really mean for policy-makers today.

'An indispensable counterweight to optimists and pessimists alike' **Will Hutton**

MAKING THE COMMONWEALTH MATTER – INTERIM REPORT

Kate Ford and Sunder Katwala

April 26th 1999 (50th Anniversary of Commonwealth); £4.95, plus £1 p+p.

This exciting, influential and controversial report has sparked off the most lively debate about the Commonwealth's future for many years. It shows how a more effective, equal and valued Commonwealth could connect more with its 1.6 billion people, enhancing its contribution to our multiethnic societies, to human rights and to prosperity.

'The biggest shake-up of the Commonwealth since it was set up in its present form 50 years ago' *The Independent on Sunday*

'The ideas will have to be taken seriously' *Daily Mail*

NETWORK EUROPE

Mark Leonard
in association with Clifford Chance
10th September 1999 £9.95, plus £1 p+p.

Mark Leonard sets out a radical new agenda for European reform, arguing that pro-Europeans must reshape the European debate if Europe is to be both effective and popular. Instead of the traditional federalist reform agenda, the EU should learn from successful network models of business organisation and introduce elements of direct democracy to reconnect to its citizens.

'A welcome contribution to the important debate about Europe's future' **Rt Hon Tony Blair MP, Prime Minister**

'A radical agenda for reform from the government's favourite foreign policy think-tank' Stephen Castle, *Independent on Sunday*

REINVENTING THE COMMONWEALTH – Final Project Report

Kate Ford and Sunder Katwala
November 8th 1999, £9.95, plus £1 p+p.

This final project report builds on the influential interim report, *Making the Commonwealth Matter*, to set out the new reform agenda for a 21st century Commonwealth. The report will be launched in South Africa in November when Commonwealth Heads of Government meet for the final time this century, determined to demonstrate that the Commonwealth is modern, relevant and looking firmly to the future. The report looks at how the Commonwealth could make this a reality – addressing the central issues of good governance, growth and global consensus, and the institutional and cultural challenges involved in reinventing the Commonwealth.

Forthcoming publications

NEW VISIONS FOR EUROPE: A Mission Statement for the EU
in association with Clifford Chance
November 24th 1999, £2.95, plus £1 p+p

The Foreign Policy Centre sets out a Mission Statement for the European Union ahead of its Millennial Declaration, outlining a new European Dream and clear goals which the European Union should commit itself to in the next five years. The mission statement will be launched at a major European conference in November.

EXPORTING VALUES: Lessons from Russia
John Lloyd
£9.95, plus £1 p+p.

Russia was the biggest laboratory for the western policy of imposing democracy and markets. But Russian hostility towards the west is now greater than at any time since Gorbachev began the reform process. What went wrong? And how do we learn the lessons? Attempting to impose capitalism without regard for local conditions or sensibilities has delivered only economic failure and political turmoil. The risk now is that the west will disengage, especially as the blame for losing Russia is becoming an issue in the US Presidential campaign. John Lloyd argues that Europe must now take the lead on a new constructive strategy if we are not to get Russian policy disastrously wrong again, and argues that we can learn important lessons for making internationalism effective elsewhere.

BRITAIN AS EUROPE
Linda Colley
£9.95, plus £1 p+p.

The leading historian of British identity shows that Eurosceptic myths of 'Europe and Britain' as separate and monolithic distort Britain's long European history, and misrepresent the nature of Continental Europe in the past and today.

MODERNISING ISLAM

Ziauddin Sardar

£9.95, plus £1 p+p.

This timely, contoversial and challenging report argues that the Muslim diaspora, far from being a threat and mere agent of a global Islamic fundamentalist agenda, can play a positive role in updating Islam.

AFTER MULTICULTURALISM

Yasmin Alibhai-Brown

£9.95, plus £1 p+p.

Yasmin Alibhai-Brown argues that we need to fundamentally rethink our approach to national identity, race and public culture. The old debate about multiculturalism no longer illuminates the new challenges for reinventing identity and participation in a developed Britain, a plural Europe and an increasingly interdependent world. We need to leave behind a debate about "ethnic minorities", which has too often only engaged blacks and asians rather than whites as well, if the coming battles over political culture and national identity are to have a progressive outcome.

Subscribe to The Foreign Policy Centre

From only £25 per year, you will receive the following benefits:

- FREE copy of GLOBALIZATION when you subscribe
- **At least 6** other Foreign Policy Centre publications
- **1 / 3 off** all other publications
- *Global Thinking*, The Foreign Policy Centre Quarterly Newsletter
- Regular mailings with full details of all publications and events
- **Sizeable discounts** on all Centre public events

The Foreign Policy Centre Business Partnership

The Foreign Policy Centre also runs a successful Business Partnership scheme, which aims to bring the business community to the heart of foreign policy decision-making.

For more details about this scheme, please contact Rachel Briggs, Corporate Affairs Manager on 0171 925 1804.

The Foreign Policy Centre Diplomatic Partnership

The Foreign Policy Centre Diplomatic Partnership is aimed at the key embassy players. It is an ideal way for embassies to keep up to date with the work of The Foreign Policy Centre and will provide a useful environment for ideas sharing.

Members will receive the following benefits:

- Special invitations to attend The Foreign Policy Centre annual Diplomatic Forum, which will be led by a high-profile speaker, bringing together key embassy players to address one or more of the foreign policy issues of the day
- Three free copies of every Foreign Policy Centre publication
- Three free copies of *Global Thinking*, The Foreign Policy Centre's newsletter
- VIP invitations for up to three embassy representatives to all Foreign Policy Centre public events
- Priority on Foreign Policy Centre non-public events, where places may become available

Membership of The Foreign Policy Centre Diplomatic Partnership is £500 per year.